Jean Frémon

David Hockney in Pays d'Auge

Translated by Georges Hume

Hermits United
London · Paris

Published in Great Britain by Hermits United Ltd. 2025

Translated from Jean Frémon, *David Hockney en Pays d'Auge*
(L'Échoppe, 2020)

English translation © Hermits United 2025

All rights reserved
Printed in Europe

A catalogue record for this book is available from the British Library
ISBN 978-1-916658-12-7

www.hermits-united.com

David Hockney in Pays d'Auge

9 October 2018.

David Hockney is spending a few days at Ferme Saint-Siméon. Just before, he was in London for the inauguration of his large stained-glass window at Westminster Abbey. He avoids three-day intercontinental trips these days, but does not wish to linger in London, where he knows he will be inundated with visitors once they hear he is in town. His solution is to flee – a car ride through the Channel Tunnel, not even stopping for lunch, just a ham-and-butter sandwich in the car. Leaving at 9 a.m., he and Jean-Pierre arrive in Honfleur by 4 p.m., in time to take in the sumptuous spectacle of the sun setting between the Pont de Normandie and the docks of Le Havre from a terrace overlooking the estuary. The sun is behind us, in the hills above Honfleur; it filters through the forest and illuminates the estuary with shifting shades. The bridge cables shine like the dewy threads of a spiderweb. For one hour, two hours, the entire duration of the spectacle, Hockney gazes at the gradual withdrawal of colours, the multitude of greys, the expansion of shadows. He comments: this or that façade is lit up, then dims; horizon lines fade, each replaced by one closer; the cables of the Pont de Normandie vanish into the twilight. We agree to meet the next day to go to Bayeux. David once saw the tapestry in 1967 and dearly wishes to see it again.

The next day, we have lunch at mine in Beuvron-en-Auge. He seems to like the house. He takes a long look around. 'You clearly know how to live', he says, then adds, 'If only I could have a place like this, I'd come to paint *The Arrival of Spring in Normandy*. That's what I'd want to do.'

We leave for Bayeux. When David enters the museum, he spots a wheelchair and takes possession of it. He can walk without the slightest difficulty, but favours his comfort; it is J.P. who pushes him. We are alone, or almost, proceeding at our own pace, and speak without anyone in earshot to bother. I do my best to decipher and translate the Latin, as we have refused the audio guides, which impose a particular rhythm and interpretation, hampering private conversations and precluding backtracking.

Hockney likens this unique example of graphic narration to the Chinese scrolls he has studied at length. In both cases, there are no shadows to be seen. A shadow halts time. A shadow results from the light of an instant; it pertains to photography, indicating space but not the passage of time. If you wish to tell a story like William's conquest of England, you need the element of time, unrolling it from left to right. Shadows are of no use here and would only complicate the narration. Narration favours profiles, whose efficacy highlights the direction of the action, as in the bas-reliefs at Luxor.

No shadows and no perspective. Only one concession: the horses' legs in the background are embroidered in a different tint to those in the foreground. Like shadow, vanishing points bring movement to a halt. Here, everything should lead us to the outcome. Dives, from which William's fleet sets out, is to the left, while Hastings, where his warriors defeat Harold, is to the right. The direction of the story here told is the direction of history. To create the impression of distance on the sea that the warriors and their horses are crossing, all one needs is to place a few smaller boats above the larger ones.

David examines, dissects, analyses. His thirst to see and to understand is palpable.

Upon our return, we drink champagne on the terrace as we watch the cinematic sunset once more. We never tire of it. His next exhibition is at the Van Gogh Museum in Amsterdam, in February. David speaks of Van Gogh, of his desire for light, his compulsive hard work – 800 paintings in just a few short years – and the popular belief about his poverty. 'A man who uses three tubes for a bit of sky is not poor', he says. 'He lived at inns, ate at bistros, always had enough money to buy his materials without calculating his expenses. Ten years later, he would have been very rich.'

*

The notion of painting springtime in Normandy is gaining ground. David and J.P. spend the next three days looking for a house in the vicinity. There is one in the hills above Rumesnil, just five minutes from us. It is a big, timbered, seventeenth-century house overlooking the valley. The driveway is lined with apple trees and, downhill from a vast meadow, poplars stand in a row along a watercourse. Beyond this stream, the hill rises again and cows graze on the slope. There is a shaded arbour in front of a pond with croaking frogs. A few dozen metres from the house stands a barn, or an old cidery, which could be turned into a vast studio after a little renovation. The deal is sealed. David returns to Los Angeles satisfied. The rendezvous is fixed for the spring, after Amsterdam. He intends to stay until June, to paint hawthorns and reread Proust. He is so excited, even rejuvenated, by his new resolution.

***

12 December 2018, Los Angeles.

The GPS – without which we would no longer know how to orient ourselves – guides us along a different path than the one David suggests on the map he has drawn, which he faxes to his visitors. We go directly up to Mulholland Boulevard from Santa Monica Boulevard, via North Crescent Drive, then to Woodrow Wilson and Montcalm Avenue. David welcomes us at his studio door – he is on top form. The large back wall is covered by a gigantic enlargement of Bruegel's *Tower of Babel*. David and J.P.

were recently in Vienna to see the Bruegel exhibition at the Kunsthistorisches Museum. Curious to study the details, David had an approximately 4 x 4 m blown-up photograph made. The centre of the painting is at eye level, where horse-drawn carts progress up the slope towards the porch by which one enters the tower.

'Look at all these different perspectives', he says. 'From here, you look down at King Nimrod's arrival and at the stonecutters kneeling in front of him; they are closer to us, but smaller than the king and his retinue – a sign of humility. In the distance, you see that little town with houses and roofs tightly nestled amongst each other, topped off by a vast countryside horizon and a flock of flying birds.' In the painting itself, of which a full-scale reproduction has been placed nearby on the floor, the birds are just minute black brushstrokes, yet with an astonishingly perfect curvature and proportion. To the right, towards the bottom, is the harbour where rafts unload building materials; infinitesimal white trimmings represent tiny waves. It is a miracle to discover all of these tiny characters busy at work in the enlarged reproduction. Two figures carry a heavy load on boards – you can recognise their suffering by their hunched backs and bent knees. A man holds out a hen that he is taking home to pluck its feathers. We distinguish only the back of another man, kneeling at the bottom of the tower: his breeches down, he gives back to the soil what the soil has given to him.

At the other end of the studio is another blown-up image David has had made. It is an enlargement of the little town on the left side of the tower. 'Look', he says, 'it's like Cézanne. All these roofs, these geometric planes heading in all directions – Cubism is already there.'

Recent portraits on canvas hang on the studio's large side wall. Charcoal drawings with white backgrounds, a little colour on the clothing, pencil and whitewash too, and beautiful light; life-sized models, all sitting in the same armchair – J.P. and Jonathan amongst them. Here is John Richardson, dated 18 August. 'How is he doing?' 'Very well', replies David, 'he is ninety-four and finishing the fourth volume of his *Picasso*.' I mention Lucian Freud's extraordinary portrait of him. 'Do you know what the Queen of England, John Richardson and I have in common?' David asks. 'We are the only people whose portraits have been painted by both

Lucian Freud and Andy Warhol.' Lucian Freud is famous for requiring his models to sit for limitless amounts of time. Hockney seeks speed, clarity, and lightness, whereas Freud dives into the drama (as does Bacon, but by other means). Hockney plays with the surface, with the impalpable. Freud does not paint skin but rather flesh, as if he were penetrating it; and the more thickness he adds, the deeper he goes inside. 'Difficult to do that with Elizabeth II', remarks David. 'She has the finest skin imaginable, like the surface of a pearl. Her face has probably never been touched by sunlight. Everyone who has been exposed to sunlight in their youth ends up with a crocodile hide.'

'When Freud did my portrait', says Hockney, 'he began with this part', pointing to his eyes and the wings of his nose. 'Then he dug, persisted, penetrated. I saw his eyes staring here', showing me his right cheek, 'seeking the flesh under the skin.'

I ask David how much time he had spent painting the portraits on the wall. 'Two sessions, each about three and a half hours. You need to work fast if you want to capture an expression, which is fleeting by its very nature.'

For lunch, fish pie. Our conversation turns around

the forgotten artist Albert Marquet. Hockney recalls his 1975 exhibition at the Jeu de Paume. He lived at the time on the Cour de Rohan, and would walk down to the Seine via rue Dauphine, where Marquet lived, overlooking the Pont Neuf. For several long minutes, he tried to remember the name of rue Dauphine, which he finally recalled, all by himself, with relief. Once again, I am struck by Hockney's infallible memory – a memory of what he has seen, read, and heard; of dates, places, and people. This surely results from his ability to observe – a constant practice that is anything but foreign to his work.

***

23 February 2019.

Unable to attend the preview of the exhibition *Hockney / Van Gogh: The Joy of Nature* in Amsterdam, I arrive the weekend before. Quite luckily, as it turns out, because David and Gregory are awaiting me for a private visit of the monumental Rembrandt exhibition celebrating the 350th anniversary of his death. The museum has brought together all of the Rembrandts it houses, several hundred drawings and engravings, as well as a few crucial paintings.

All those little engravings, no bigger than postage stamps... There was a market for them, as the art historian accompanying us explains: expressing such precise sentiments on such a small surface with only a chisel and aqua fortis was a feat that the public appreciated.

David: 'Back then, they had much better eyesight than we do. Their eyesight was not damaged by artificial lighting. Not to mention the screens that are everywhere today. I always wear a cap to protect my eyes from too much brightness.'

*

David: 'Rembrandt put more into a head than anyone else. Except perhaps Van Gogh...'

*

David: 'Rembrandt gave this advice to his students: "Don't travel, not even to Italy." This reminds me of Beckett's quip: "We don't travel for the fun of it, as far as I know; we're foolish, but not that foolish."'

*

Rembrandt: A mother holds a young boy to help him pee. David uses his mobile phone to look up an image: it is the same subject, drawn by Picasso. He points out that the hands in Picasso's drawing can be seen much better than in Rembrandt's. 'Cubism is about closeness', he adds.

*

Later on, again about Rembrandt: '"A woman making water" – nice way of putting it. The stream of piss is a ray of light.'

*

He is amused by a small engraving that depicts a monk with his cassock raised, fondling a peasant woman at the base of a haystack. I'm the one who calls her a peasant woman, though nothing indicates this. Hockney: 'She must be a nun.'

*

A small rectangular horizontal engraving: a man with two dogs heading towards a village; in the background, a bell tower and an imposing hill. 'Where can such a hill be found in this flat country?' asks David. Our host confirms that it is not a real hill, but an imaginary one that provides a background to buttress the scene. Reality is a pretext, not a goal; the goal is the painting. One has no obligation to reality; to the painting, one owes probity.

*

A delicious dinner at Seafood Bar, where we order the same meal: oysters and sole meunière. When I say that I prefer my sole dry, David exclaims: 'I want butter!' He has invited two young artists to dine with us, the Oakes Brothers, twins who work together. One of them conceives the painting, the other executes it. They show us an example of their work on a mobile phone: a view of the half-frozen Hudson River. Every day, for 11 days, the twins' 'hand' paints the landscape in front of them on a narrow vertical strip. The next day, another vertical strip is painted with the same proportions, contiguous to the preceding one; the structure of the landscape is strictly identical, but the light has changed, for the sky has cleared up or become cloudy. In brief, the landscape remains stable but time does not, and the painting records its passing. The painted image coincides perfectly with the margins of the landscape stretching beyond the painting, so that hardly any difference can be discerned between what is real and what is figured. One understands what has drawn Hockney's attention to this experiment, and why these two young artists consider him a master.

*

The following day, we set out to see the exhibition at the Van Gogh Museum. The institution has been transformed into a giant touristic factory, with extensions creating a vast underground space occupied by the Temple merchants. Every floor of the exhibition opens with a kind of staging of aggrandised documents and photographs of the master's drawings. It is Disneyland.

Fortunately, the exhibition itself remains at a slight remove from this circus. Bringing Hockney and Van Gogh together is a legitimate choice. The two oeuvres coincide in numerous ways, and

Hockney's art contains outright borrowings and tributes: the singularity of brushstrokes that fit the form, the powerful colours, a sense of space freed from conventions, not to mention chairs... As it turns out, the catalogue takes this relationship into account much better than the exhibition itself does. Many of Van Gogh's works in the catalogue are not included in the exhibition. The catalogue also enables reproductions of the two artists' works to be set side by side on the same scale, whereas Hockney's paintings are generally much larger than Van Gogh's.

*

Once the festivities of the preview are over, Jean-Pierre picks David up in Amsterdam and drives him back to Rumesnil, where the house is ready for him to live in and the new studio is almost fully restored. This is where we join them on 17 March. What a transformation! The former cidery, cluttered with old roof beams, has been entirely emptied and insulated. The timbered walls have been doubled inside and repainted white. A new wooden floor has been laid. Skylights bring in light from above. There is a place to rest, and a kitchenette at the back; and above these, a mezzanine on which printers, cameras, computers, and all the other technology managed by Jonathan have been set up.

David has begun drawing on a leporello, a 24-page accordion of a book. He has outlined what he sees outside the house in India ink and red chalk. But the singularity of this drawing – the lesson of the Bayeux Tapestry is already present – is that EVERYTHING outside the house can be seen: out front, out back, to the left, to the right. Linking every new view to the previous one, he goes all the way around the house; if you do not know the place, you couldn't tell that the house is at the centre. The sketchbook is thus a walk, a circumvolution, a loop whose two extremities join up. I ask David if he made a map of everything in order to determine the scale that would allow the whole loop to be contained within the 24 pages. He answers no. He began by drawing what was in front of him, and then gradually moved around the house, drawing all the while; as if by chance, he had come full circle at the end of the sketchbook. Some people have perfect pitch, Hockney has a perfect sense of scale.

*

Didier Ottinger offers Hockney the possibility of a Matisse-Hockney exhibition at the Matisse Museum. It is a magnificent theme. On his computer, David shows us Ottinger's workplan and the visual comparisons he intends to implement.

Kevin, Jean-Pierre's nephew, is here; it is he Hockney painted as a sailor when, one day while on leave, he had come to visit his uncle without taking off his official Marine Nationale uniform. David made two large portraits of him on his iPad. It is impossible not to notice similarities between these and Matisse's young sailor at the Metropolitan Museum in New York. David recalls seeing it in the collection of its former owners, Jacques and Natasha Gelman, in Mexico City. Kevin and Matisse's sailor have the same tapered eyes; their respective poses on the chair are different, but one cannot look at Hockney's painting without Matisse's re-emerging.

***

31 March 2019.

David has set an appointment with me for 3 p.m. The day is almost summery. The renovation worksite has considerably changed since the last time. The scaffolding has been taken down and the mezzanine stairway installed. Outside, benches and deckchairs can be found nearly everywhere around the house. A large wooden terrace that overlooks the stream below has been built in front of the studio. I join David, who is sporting his cap, in the house, and he immediately leads me to the studio. 16 big drawings, about 70 x 100 cm in size, have been placed against a wall. It is the same subject as the leporello – that is, the walk around the house – but enlarged. He needs to make eight more to come full circle. He has drawn in colour inks, as in the leporello, and used watercolours with a brush whenever stronger marks are needed. The result is more colourful than the initial leporello, with more details, a multitude of little graphic inventions, Pointillism, curving Van Gogh-like marks. The season is progressing, colours are emerging. A 360-degree panoramic view with neither shadows nor a vanishing point. Nothing like it has ever been seen in Western art. 'Well, it's not reality, it's an image', he says. 'The leporello helped me to put everything in place. Now I'm freer, I make progress faster, I know my subject.' As we walk around the house, he shows me the parts omitted from his depiction, generally for compositional reasons: a barrier around the pond, for example, which would have blocked the view and disturbed the reflections – that he has painted in blue, with obvious pleasure – of the branches in the water. I ask if he will paint the house after painting everything surrounding it. 'Of course. The artists of this region, the Impressionists, did not often paint this type of timbered Norman house, a vestige of the sixteenth century that can be found in Rembrandt's drawings. The Impressionists were looking for modernity instead of the "old France", so they favoured harbours, metallic bridges, and factory chimneys over traditional houses. They must have thought the latter looked like fairy-tale houses, and that frightened them. As for me, I'm not afraid of painting them.' How long does he intend to stay in Normandy? 'As long as the work goes well. I went to Bridlington for four weeks and ended up staying nine years.'

***

5 April 2019.

A quick visit to see how the work is progressing.

The 24th drawing is underway. Only a few more days remain before I will be able to admire this great panorama: what I see when walking around the house. The last building, because of the shape of its roof, finely rounds out the group. David comes back to his idea that the timbered walls of Norman houses have rarely been depicted by painters. Is it because this motif did not seem serious? As if it were the house of Snow White and the Seven Dwarfs? Didier Ottinger has not shied from pointing out common denominators between Hockney and Walt Disney. In any case, Hockney shows no disdain for Disney; on the contrary, he respects this man who knew how to make an image that was simple, efficacious, and memorable.

'I've spent a week on all that green down there', he says. 'All those marks gave me a terrible time.' He is speaking about the gravel driveway and the lawn. As often happens, Hockney's marks appear abstract and freely drawn when examined up close, but create a strong illusion of reality once one stands back. Yesterday, I was at the Musée des Beaux-Arts in Rouen, which was exhibiting a selection of Braque's landscapes of Varengeville – those small, oblong canvases with the sky, the ground, a plough or two boats on the beach. Thinking of Hockney, I examined the inventiveness visible in the choice of marks representing the pebbly beach. A Pointillism turned Expressionist re-emerges in Braque in his last years. The Musée des Beaux-Arts in Le Havre is preparing a Dufy exhibition, as I learn from its curator, a woman whom I met in Rouen. 'Dufy', says Hockney, 'a great inventor of marks. People have been unjust to him. As they have been to Marquet!'

'To bring time into painting, horizontality is needed. Jean Renoir would complain that filmmaking was vertical and halted time.' 'It's perhaps because of this', I observe, 'that he kept his characters on the move. This is evident in *The Rules of the Game*, in which no one stays put and the characters keep running into each other like billiard balls.' 'And in Tati', adds David, 'when one character leaves the screen to the left, another arrives from the right – it's fascinating.' Hockney is a great fan of Jean Renoir and Jacques Tati, formidable animators of flat surfaces.

He places the leporello in front of the 24 large drawings and we compare them. Many colours have appeared: the blue reflections of the pond (the sky must have been clear that day); the flowers of the big pear tree, which were not in bloom when the leporello was made, but which are now cottony white; three cars in the courtyard, which will one day date this drawing. Hockney has no fear of contemporaneity, he seizes hold of it. A phone charger plugged into a socket? He draws it. An ashtray full of cigarette butts? He draws it. And why not? He draws what he sees out of a concern for the truth of what he is. Having nothing to hide about himself, he has nothing to hide about what he sees, nor about what he loves. Indeed, he loves to paint what he sees.

***

7 April 2019.

Catherine Cusset and her husband come to see us, then we have an aperitif at David's house. He liked her book, the American translation of which has just appeared. I take them all to dinner at the Grand Hôtel in Cabourg. I show David the sentence from *In the Shadow of Young Girls in Flower* where Proust describes workers walking past the restaurant and peering at the bourgeois customers inside, as if they were fish in an aquarium. The hotel has had this sentence engraved on a plaque attached to a signpost on the boardwalk, facing the sea. We enter the aquarium. 'This would no longer be true today', remarks David. 'No such display of hats and finery exists anymore, as it did in the last century. We dress like yesteryear's workers. Excepting the Yellow Vests.' He continues: 'I have never been tempted by communism. Communism lures with a promise of the future. I don't want to live in the future, nor for the future – I want to live now. Some people live in the past, others in the future. I want to live in the now.' He reiterates his wish to reread *In Search of Lost Time*. He is currently reading a biography of Oscar Wilde, and seems to enjoy it greatly.

***

14 April 2019.

Jean-Pierre is ill. David is alone in the studio. I find him sitting and scrutinising the watercolour of La Grande Cour from afar: 24 sheets of paper, each clipped to a piece of rigid cardboard and placed next to one another on the large wall of the studio, long enough to accommodate this arrangement. Hockney's main activity seems to be looking: looking at nature, looking at his friends, looking at paintings, patiently, for a long time, until he finds where he can put that darker line, giving more relief to an object – here, the garden swing. Since last week, he has added hills far to the right, and this prolongs the drawing, giving it distance and depth. 'I have added a few trees here and there', he says. 'And flowers that were not in bloom when I began.' The passage of time is the main theme – each thing before our eyes has its inscription in time: the hills have always been there; the barn for a century or two; the trees for a few decades; the flowers, which have just blossomed on the pear tree and on the apple trees, will last only a few days; the irises around the pond, which had not yet sprouted from the ground when he was drawing the leporello, are now in the large watercolour drawing. But what goes by even more quickly in time is not there: the clouds in the sky. Hockney has decided to keep the sky white in the watercolour, for this nicely suits the still, wintery atmosphere of the landscape. Most of the trees are still leafless, and the whole maintains a simplified graphic character, a restrained use of colour; a cloudy sky – or even an utterly blue one, as it has mostly been this week – would disturb the neat, purified aspect that he intends to maintain for his composition, one that stands out against the whiteness of the paper. But all the same, when I remarked that he had not painted the sky, he spontaneously replied: 'It changes too quickly.' Missing as well, for the same reason, are the white-hoofed horses that we glimpsed in the distant meadow beyond the stream, below the house, when we had our sunset aperitif with Catherine Cusset. Likewise, there is no bird on the lawn, in a tree, or in the sky; time for the tree and time for the bird are not the same.

*

I have brought an early painting I have purchased – *Portrait of John Sharp*, 1953 – with the thought that he might be happy to see it again, which is the case. He examines it for a long time and points out that the model looks out of only one eye, and this he does sideways. I had hoped that he could tell me about the person in the portrait, but he cannot recall. 'I was sixteen', he says. The model is wearing a large white apron. 'Possibly a cook', he suggests.

I have also brought a photograph of a drawing: a nude portrait in ink of Gregory, made in one line – a marvel of delicacy, the art of taking shortcuts, a prodigious fusion in a single stroke of observed reality: the contours of a naked body and the expression of an emotion, the painter's love for his model. He says: 'Single-line drawings are the most difficult, because you need to hold intense concentration to draw slowly. You can't second guess. And between these two lines imitating a form, you must sense a volume where there is only white paper.'

***

4 May 2019.

David tells me over the phone that he is returning to London tomorrow to have lunch with the Queen. He describes her as a friendly, cultivated woman, and an avid reader. He likes her reedy voice. From there, he and Jean-Pierre will go to Los Angeles for three weeks to renew their green cards. As it turns out, the panorama of La Grande Cour will be shown at the opening of the new Pace Gallery building in New York. David, who had first proposed it to me, begs my pardon. He specifies that it will not be sold in

New York and adds that he has several painting projects planned for his return here this summer, announcing his desire to show these works made in France at an exhibition in Paris. He is expecting me at 6 p.m.

I arrive at his studio at 6 p.m. sharp. David is sitting in a wheelchair, which enables him to move, without getting tired, by using his feet in front of him. He has made five large watercolours of the house and of the adjoining garden viewed from different angles since my last visit. More precisely, he has been working on exactly that which could not be seen in the leporello nor in its transposition into a large format: the heart of the panorama. Free, fluid, vigorous touches. Chinese-style, without shadows. There is still no sky, but nor is there any restriction of colours as in the first leporello; it was still almost winter here back then, and spring has exploded since. What he seeks is obvious: the surging forth of life, surging forth in him at the same time as in nature. A little treehouse sits in the big pear tree in bloom behind the house. It is approximately two metres up from the ground and can be reached by a ladder, but no one risks doing so. At the base of the pear tree, a hawthorn bush is also about to blossom.

A sudden schedule change: they will indeed go to London tomorrow to have lunch with the Queen, but they will come back on Wednesday. The reason? 'I'm not going to miss the blossoming of the hawthorns; it's just started – when we get back, they'll be in full bloom. All the hedges here have them, and I must paint them. We'll go to Los Angeles later.' The moral of a life lies in the priorities one determines for oneself.

Reproductions of the most recent watercolours hang on the wall. They are twice the size of the originals, which have left for New York. I ask David why he feels the need to print enlargements of his work. 'It makes my hand bigger', he says. He can study each mark from afar and learn lessons from them or make corrections. I notice that he spends more time looking at his work and thinking about it – in order to improve it, to make it more striking, simpler, more self-evident – than he spends painting. He not only has enlargements made, but also reductions. The first leporello was printed in a very small format and folded, like the original sketchbook, into a minuscule book. Larger, smaller, unfolded, refolded... He studies all the possibilities, analyses their visual impact.

After a glass of white wine in the house, and with the sun now shining, he decrees that we will take a reconnaissance tour in the vicinity by car, to search for the hawthorn bushes that he plans to paint next week. Driving slowly, we explore the nearby roads; he observes everything, both scouting locations and soaking up the landscape.

***

1 June 2019.

Michel Serres has died. He was commenting on current affairs on television only a few days ago. When the journalist asked him to react to any of the news items that had just been reeled off, Serres said, 'But you announce only bad news.' The journalist retorted, 'Do you happen to know of any good news?' 'I do', answered the philosopher. 'For example?' 'Well, for example, the arrival of spring.'

David Hockney listens to this story with a satisfied smile.

***

24 June 2019.

David has written a short text for the catalogue that will accompany the exhibition opening at Pace Gallery in September. He asks me to translate it. Here is the original:

The work started as a reproduction of Bruegel's Tower of Babel. I had made it 12 feet high, so you had to look all over it. You looked down on the sea. You looked up to see the top of the tower. It is full of different perspectives. I thought it was almost like a new painting.

I then left for Amsterdam, where I saw Rembrandt and Van Gogh. Bruegel, Rembrandt and Van Gogh all drew landscapes with great clarity, 'extra crispy and clear', a friend said.

I arrived in Normandy on March 2nd. The studio wouldn't be finished until the end of the month, so I started drawing on a book I had bought in Amsterdam. It was a Japanese concertina book, and I started on March 4th and worked all around the house, finishing it on March 16th. I then began it again, this time bigger, with more detail.

The work has no vanishing point, but unlike Chinese or Japanese art, it has few shadows (under the cars) and a reflection in the pond. It is drawn in the Chinese way. It is not a window. I actually walked all around the house, why not?

I am sometimes amazed that European art historians do not know that shadows or reflections do not occur in Chinese or Japanese art. Indeed, only the Europeans used them.

It took me 21 days to make the 24 drawings. All of my marks are visible, thousands of them. I was able to finish the drawing in my new high-tech studio. Being in the studio, seeing its straight lines, I decided to draw our higgledy-piggledy house, also from the north, south, east and west.

My plan is to do The Arrival of Spring *like the Bayeux Tapestry, i.e., you walk past it. The Bayeux Tapestry is a great work of art, made in 1100 (eleven hundred). It contains no shadows or reflections. So when did they start using them in Europe? This has long been a question of mine. It covers about four years of time, so it is made like a Chinese scroll. A window would be no use here.*

The arrival of spring takes about six weeks in Normandy, so I intend to do it like a scroll. It's a movie, but you do the moving.

David Hockney, June 2019

When I gave him my French translation, David immediately looked to see how I had translated 'higgledy-piggledy house'. I still hear him pronouncing 'de bric et de broc' in order to experience the sound.

The last sentence in my translation, 'C'est comme un film mais c'est vous qui vous déplacez', does not have the same quality as in English, as the idea of movement is not present in the word 'film'.

***

14 July 2019.

Jean-Pierre has taken a few days off and Jonathan has gone to Paris to pick up his wife and daughter, who are arriving from Bradford. I find David sitting alone at the table recently placed on the wooden terrace next to the studio. He is wearing a grey suit and a white cap, and pores over a small sketchbook that he then holds out to me, inviting me to leaf through it. These are the drawings he made in Los Angeles during his brief stay there for administrative reasons. The drawings extend over the double horizontal page of the sketchbook – a cinematographic proportion that suits him well, even in a small format. This proportion is also narrative, by which I mean that it naturally unfolds from left to right and gives the impression of telling a story; abandoned is the snapshot from the traditional window. Views of the garden as if made at ground level, the cacti along the path, pure lines, without shadows, Matisse-like outlines, portraits, Bing, Gregory... a few drawings after Rembrandt... The sketchbook ends with a black-and-white landscape observed on the road to Lisieux and the very last one is of the table around which we are now sitting, at the centre of which stands a porcelain pot from Morocco, used as an ashtray. No background, only the foreground of the table, the back of a chair, and this porcelain pot. All of this is depicted at the exact distance from the painter sitting at the end of the table, which he draws.

'Bruegel, Rembrandt, and Van Gogh drew landscapes of great clarity', he says. I lament the absence of Van Gogh's ink drawings at the exhibition in Amsterdam. The museum only shows them on privately arranged visits because they are so fragile. Hockney has had the privilege of examining them in the drawers where they are kept. It is in the drawings, more than the paintings, that the proximity between Van Gogh and Hockney is the most evident: the distinct, separate marks, multiplied until they end up forming an openwork surface that is life itself. The white paper between the ink marks lets the drawing breathe. He approves: 'In pen and ink drawings, each mark can be seen autonomously. Rembrandt also made pen and ink drawings.' We enter the studio, where a big Rembrandt album lies open on a lectern. The enlargement of Breughel's *Tower of Babel* is still on the back wall. Hockney lives surrounded by the works of the painters he admires; they are not always the same ones, and Picasso often returns, but they are always master draughtsmen – the substance of the matter. At the moment, everything revolves around Bruegel, Rembrandt, and Van Gogh.

A new watercolour shows the gable of the house as viewed from the studio. 'This drawing seems very spontaneous, doesn't it? But it isn't. I drew the sky first – nothing but the sky and the big white clouds rising and standing out in the sky. I let two days go by and then I added blue and red. The blue is the indecisive blue-spotted line on the horizon, the red is the house's tile roof. Those blue spots on the horizon are probably the hedge that marks off the property; the hedge isn't blue, it's green, but the blue beckons the eye deeply into the background. I then let the drawing sit for three more days, during which I did other things, but I didn't stop thinking about it. In fact, I thought about nothing else. At the end, I did the trees to the left and right, and the green lines of the freshly cut grass.' And probably, in the process, the house timbers, green here for the first time, are depicted with wide, vertical, roughly parallel marks made with a paintbrush; but there are no windows. 'The timbers are obviously not green in reality – so what? Nor is the hedge blue, but the drawing works this way. The leaves of the trees are made with scattered dots on the white paper. I like each mark to be visible.' There is no second guessing, but much thinking between each mark, and no getting carried away emotionally. Expressing spontaneity demands restraint and precise gestures.

We are sitting on the terrace, facing the subject of the watercolour. Between the painting of the watercolour and today, the neighbouring farmer has made hay. Big cylindrical yellow-green bales lie scattered here and there. The sunlight makes their smooth surface shine. The haystacks that Monet painted – built up expertly by hand and pitchfork – are no more; today, agricultural machines – those enormous insects with their huge pincers – lay their eggs about the fields. As a cloud passes by, the shiny surface of the balls of hay suddenly darkens and becomes matt.

***

29 July 2019.

David shows me a sketchbook full of views of the village square in Beuvron. One of them, extending over a double page, depicts the two rows of houses flaring out from the central market hall. Once again, he has apprehended space as no one else can. He tells me that this drawing was done from memory, not from nature. It is indeed quite abstract, freely drawn with respect to reality, and re-composed. It has been done from memory, but only after making several on-the-spot sketches in notebooks. He intends to make a two-panel painting from this drawing, but for the time being, he is working on a single large watercolour of the same subject.

The impressionists rarely painted Norman houses.

They painted the sea, the cliffs, the countryside, the haystacks, the poplars, the beaches, even the cows. In Le Havre, the Musée des Beaux-Arts is full of Boudin's small paintings with three cows under a tree, but those typical timbered, thatched- or tile-roof houses are absent. Some Pont-Aven artists depicted houses, but granite ones. The houses here are not very different in essence from those we see in Rembrandt's drawings and engravings that constantly inspire Hockney. Most of the old timbered houses date from the sixteenth century and the others imitate them. David: 'Actually, up to now, only amateur painters have dared to paint such subjects. Because they are too picturesque?

'They say that painting is dead, but painting and drawing will last as long as singing and dancing. And people will always sing and dance, even during a war or the worst times.'

From his trip to Amsterdam, he has brought back a large reproduction of a Van Gogh drawing showing the courtyard of the Arles asylum. The reproduction has been placed on a lectern in the studio. The enlargement enables one to clearly distinguish each pen mark. This is what interests David Hockney: studying each mark, understanding its exactness, its vigour. Understanding how the artist places his hand and then withdraws it. Learning by looking, indefatigably.

The big Taschen album of Rembrandt's drawings is also on a lectern. The enormous blow-up of Bruegel's painting, which fills the back wall, is now mostly covered by Hockney's new paintings. Van Gogh and Rembrandt remain daily companions.

*

At dinner, inside the house, he sits across from a lithographic triptych by Bacon. 'I saw Bacon just after George Dyer's death in Paris, at the preview of the exhibition at the Grand Palais. I expressed my condolences. He replied: "What can one do, except laugh or weep – no?" Then he burst out in sinister theatrical laughter.

'Bacon was somewhat snobbish. I had done my parents' portrait, which he considered a typical petit-bourgeois subject. Lucian Freud was the little brother. But when his star began to rise, Bacon took umbrage.'

I ask David what he does in the evening. In Los Angeles, he often watches a series on Netflix, but he has no television here. He replies: 'I think about what I've done during the day and what I'll do tomorrow. You need to think all the time about what you are painting. You need to think about it exclusively. Nothing good has ever been done in any other way. All the time that I spend thinking about what I will do the next day means time saved, solutions found, choices made.'

***

31 July 2019.

I have just received an e-mail with a photograph of the large watercolour of the village square. I say watercolour for the sake of simplicity, but the term is inexact: it is a coloured ink drawing. The hills appear beyond the roofs. The sky is now present. Every morning, he goes to the square and draws a new view in his sketchbook; it is his way of learning, of becoming acquainted with all of the details before plunging into the painting. Obviously, in an acrylic painting, the marks differ from those made in ink; a paintbrush does not make the same mark as a pen. And the scale is different. But with his new habit of having blow-ups made of sketchbook pages or medium-sized ink drawings, he constantly faces issues of scale and the relationship between the mark, the movement of the arm, and the size of the image. All of these questions find their resolution in larger-format paintings.

***

4 August 2019.

David shows me the sketchbook he had begun while in Los Angeles and finished in Beuvron. He has had it doubled in size, then put back together as a sketchbook. This second version remains of a size at which his hand could easily have drawn it. I ask: 'Because you like to have a bigger sketchbook, why not make it bigger from the onset?' 'For practical reasons', he replies. 'The small sketchbook is of a size that perfectly fits my pocket. I take it with me everywhere. I can take it out at any moment and sketch what I see. But by blowing up the drawing, I can better see each mark my hand has made. I can examine all of them with a fresh mind, learning from them for another drawing, another painting.'

He has placed the enlarged sketchbook upright on the table and turns each page for me. We are sitting in front of the table, David in his wheelchair. We can move back to look from a greater distance. Most of the drawings are monochromatic, but not necessarily black. There are interior views, of the studio, of the house: the table, an armchair, a few books, the windowpane constellated with raindrops pierced by a ray of sunlight. It is a diary, the chronicle of a peaceful life nonetheless alert to the slightest distinction. On one page, a head of garlic in its little lavender plastic net. I recognise it, since I buy the same garlic at the Dozulé supermarket. Why not paint a head of garlic? But more importantly, how can the fine mesh of this little lavender net, through which the head of garlic is visible, be painted? It is good to take on every challenge. It is impossible to draw each of the small marks forming the uncountable, more or less crushed diamonds of the plastic net that holds the garlic. As always, the solution lies in graphic inventiveness, the freedom of the marks and yet their faithfulness to a vision of the whole. On the lefthand page of the sketchbook, Hockney has written: *Ail blanc*.

'Art schools don't teach drawing any more, and

that's indeed regrettable', he says. 'I learned rather quickly because I had an undeniable talent for it. But first you must learn to look. Obviously, if the world doesn't interest you, there is no hope...' He adds: 'I am of course aware that most people don't really look at what is in front of them. They probably have something better to do.'

He says: 'In Bridlington, we had a house by the sea. To be frank, the sea didn't interest me very much, so I had to take the car to find trees, nature, at Woldgate or in the vicinity. Here, I have everything at hand. I don't need to go out. I know now every tree, every hill. I know at what time of day this or that can be seen better. We have cherry trees, apple trees, pear trees, an apricot tree, a fig tree, a quince tree. They blossom at different times of the year. This year, I missed the spring flowering, as I was busy with the La Grande Cour panorama. But I will not let the next spring go by. The spectacle changes every day, minute by minute. The only permanent thing we've got is change.

'I love flowers and love painting them. It's said that painting flowers is old-fashioned and no longer done. But what I paint is life. Is life old-fashioned? I claim that any drawing or painting of a flower is better than the most beautiful photograph of a flower. This is because the flower is alive and what is alive can only be so in time. During the time spent drawing or painting, you can capture life. Not so with a photograph.' I bring up counterexamples: Blossfeldt, Mapplethorpe's tulips. He makes no response.

Jonathan has returned from England with his new Porsche. His fourteen-year-old son is visiting. David hastens to portray him on a sketchbook page. We take leave of one another. He heads towards the house with his sketchbook. 'I must draw the Porsche. I'll go there right away.'

The two-panel painting of the village square is underway. The proportions have changed with respect to the watercolour: in the painting, everything is enlarged. David has pinned the blown-up sketchbook pages of views of the village to the wall; using his memory and his sketches allows him to work in the peace and quiet of his studio. He takes liberties with proportions and perspectives, accentuating the circusy aspect of the square with its two streets curving around it. He is accountable only to his painting, to its presence, to its obviousness. He is faithful to nothing else. 'I'm going to add some people sitting at tables outside the restaurant and in front of the creperie.'

***

27 August 2019.

A new painting, a new subject: one of the apple trees along the driveway. It can be seen from the studio, but it is not from there that it was painted. Hockney had gone outside to sit down in front of it. Jean-Pierre had carried the easel out, set up a parasol, and brought an armchair.

Has such an apple tree ever been seen? I don't think so. It is enthroned in the middle of the canvas with its golden apples, each of them round, light yellow, encircled in a murky yellow – this is how he resolves the issues of perspective and the volume of the apples. But the real find here is how he paints the sky: hundreds of wriggling worm-like marks, all of which have the same light-blue colour but which let the white background of the canvas play between them.

'The sky was absolutely cloudless', explains David, 'a solid blue that I found boring. I needed to find a way to animate it. The first day, I left the sky empty, which was an option. That evening, I thought a lot about it in bed, to find a solution. This is the great advantage of being here in Normandy: no newspapers, no television, a few visitors; with evenings usually free, I spend my time thinking about what to do the next day. That's how I found the solution for the sky behind the apple tree. I wanted the sky to be gleaming, shimmering, glimmering. Well, that's how it is.'

'I can only imagine Van Gogh', I say, 'daring to paint such a bold background.'

A luminous smile fleetingly brightens David's eyes and mouth.

'I'm going to paint the apple tree in the autumn when it loses its leaves, then in mid-winter with another light, when it will have only its branches and trunk; then with the first buds, and I'll paint it again when it's covered with blossoms and once more with all its leaves. Then, we'll have *L'Année du pommier* – a year in the life of an apple tree, with the sense of time passing, like in the Bayeux Tapestry.'

David knows that he is broaching something he has not yet done. He senses it to be within reach, and this gives him an energy and a vigour, visible on the canvas.

'You are creating a dialogue with the great tradition of French painting', I tell him. 'A dialogue hitherto unattempted. You are rising to the challenge.'

Another smile.

We speak of Constable's landscapes. I recall the exhibition at the Grand Palais a few years ago that brought together both studies and finished paintings. The studies on canvas, with the same format as the paintings, seemed so much more modern than the paintings, which, with their slick finish, were the only ones to find favour with the public back then.

'Impressionism wouldn't have existed without the invention of tube paint', David says. 'There is often a technical invention behind aesthetic revolutions.'

Then we speak of Manet. Manet and the Japanese. Manet and perspective. The two *Asparagus* paintings commissioned by Ephrussi. The mystery of *The Balcony*.

*

David's close friend Celia – the famous Mrs Clark of the double portrait with Percy, and his lifelong model – is coming next week. David wants to add a portrait of her to the already impressive series he plans to show at the National Portrait Gallery next year. The portraits span an entire lifetime – another way of painting time. Time regained. The exhibition will be centred on the five models whom Hockney has painted the most often, over a near six-decade period: Celia, Gregory, Maurice Payne, the artist's mother, and the artist himself.

***

7 September 2019.

The paintings in progress are in the same state as during my previous visit. The week has been devoted to portraits. Four portraits of Celia, one of David's sister Margaret, and one of his niece.

On paper, with fine ink strokes, Celia is portrayed in a polka-dot dress, a ribbon tied around her neck. The dress seems made of guinea fowl feathers, as Hockney has made a great number of more or less spaced-out little white dots. Two other, rather similar portraits are in three-quarter views, with Celia wearing a kind of loose-fitting blouse and a hat. These drawings are lighter than the first one: the blouse is flowing, Cézanne-like. The fourth portrait is a front view. 'Celia didn't like it', says David. Margaret wears an ironic smile and a modest look. 'Celia is more conceited', adds David, 'and this portrait doesn't show her to her advantage. Her waistline has thickened. It's a less flattering portrait, but I can't make a flattering portrait. I have never done so.'

He has begun a new concertina book for a tour around the house. He is now at the pond. It is midsummer, the trees still have all their leaves. 'I want to do this in every season', he says.

Blown-up reproductions of the first three sketchbooks have been pinned to the wall, one atop the other. One can compare them and look for differences. In doing so, one better understands how the artist proceeds when facing reality: not everything should be kept, as though in excessive deference. If a given tree blocks the view, it can be removed to maintain the depth of field. It is like a narrative: one must synthetise, summarise, simplify – otherwise, one gets lost in detail and cannot reach the end. The image is therefore clearer than reality.

One might call this the Bayeux syndrome: is a painting on a long surface, such as a leporello or a scroll, necessarily narrative? If so, the narrative must be organised. Important points must be handled like elements in a plot, and a visual rhythm established. Farewell, old Alberti's window, for we are on a train with the landscape speeding by. It is a film.

'I have no visitors next week, so I'll be able to make progress on my paintings. I want to do the big pear tree that stands next to the apple tree. It has a few pears, so I need to do it soon. The subjects offered to me here are endless. There is no need to go out, because everything is within reach.'

***

15 September 2019.

'I'm now doing the pear tree.' The news arrives by e-mail. I dash out. The same pose as the apple tree, the same format. I say 'pose' as if it were a portrait, but this is indeed what it is: the portrait of a tree. The sky is dealt with in the same spirit: a monochromatic structure, denser and darker than for the apple tree, that makes the space vibrate.

The exhibition opens at Pace Gallery in New York with the big drawing in 24 parts and four views of the house in coloured inks. The gallery publicises the artist's new subject matter. The information, which has appeared in a few American newspapers, is immediately picked up by French newspapers. *Ouest-France* prints a headline claiming that David Hockney is fleeing Los Angeles and settling in the Bessin area. It is unclear who prints this first mistake, which is soon copied by all the other newspapers. There are reports that Hockney has personal attachments in Orne and that one of his three sons was born there. Utter nonsense. A distraught David telephones me, begging me to discourage all interview requests without even informing him of them.

Serious requests, like one made by Fabrice Hergott, who is in charge of organising an exhibition at the Frieder Burda Museum in Baden Baden, or by the filmmaker Cédric Klapisch, are thus set aside due to the excitement of the tabloid press. Klapisch, who claims that his filmmaking has been influenced by the artist, wished to converse with him on camera.

***

28 September 2019.

Intense work over the past few days. The two-panel view of Beuvron is finished. It now includes small silhouettes sitting at tables outside the Café Forges, a bistro that grills ribs in what used to be a horseshoe forge. The painting is effective. Hockney has captured the singular perspective by accentuating the curves of the two streets that go around the old market hall, which now houses a restaurant and a few antique dealers attracting Chinese tourists. There is a narrow band of sky near the top edge of the composition, like in Gauguin's paintings of Brittany; a few white clouds… Up until now, he had been hesitant about painting clouds. 'They change too quickly', he would say.

Next to the pear tree and the apple tree, each showing off their dangling fruit, he has painted a small quince tree. The three paintings have the same format and employ the same principle in dealing with the sky, which vibrates. The tree occupies the same central position in each.

Another quince tree is in progress on the easel.

To the left is a drawing in black, surely made from nature, which the artist has enlarged on the canvas. Here, the composition is different, more dynamic: the foreground is on a slope, a background has been sketched. The ground is constellated with quinces fallen to the grass. It is a vanitas. Summer is ending, the fruit is falling; soon it will be the leaves' turn.

'I'll also do them in winter', he says. 'I'll go to Los Angeles for a few weeks in December, but I want to come back here to paint the winter, then the spring, which I didn't really have time to capture this year because I was getting my bearings. Now I work much faster. I can make a sketchbook of the panorama around the house in five days; for the first one, I needed fifteen. There are already four sketchbooks and I'm going to do more. It's interesting to look at them together. They are my little Bayeux tapestries.'

At dinner, David eats with a hearty appetite, drinks only a little. He speaks of Kasmin, his first London art dealer. He says that François Pinault has offered to come and visit by helicopter. 'The last thing I want to see is a helicopter landing on our property.' He recalls that Paul Cornwall-Jones, his print publisher, had travelled to the Glyndebourne

Festival by helicopter. He was intent on showing everyone how busy he was. A little later, he went bankrupt. As soon as dinner ends, David says he is tired. 'Tomorrow I'll stay in bed.' I remind him of the sign that Saint-Pol-Roux would hang on his bedroom doorknob when he was about to take a nap: 'The poet is working.' David likes the quip. Much of his work is done in bed as he thinks of what he has done and what he is going to do.

David's assistant Shannan Kelly has come from Los Angeles for a few days. She asks how long we have known each other. It is Vera Russell who introduced me to David at the preview of his photo collage exhibition organised by Kasmin in London – I cannot remember the date. '1982', says David. He is right. I was in London with Vera to see Henry Moore, with whom I was preparing an exhibition. I remember catching glimpses of David Hockney in Paris during the 1970s. Once at a table outside Les Deux Magots, then at the preview of his exhibition at the Musée des Arts Décoratifs, then again at the preview of the Bacon exhibition at the Grand Palais in 1971. But we did not know each other then.

Soon after going into the living room for some herbal tea, he falls asleep in an armchair. He has to be wakened to go home.

***

18 October 2019.

Already a year has gone by since the visit to Bayeux and the decision to settle in Normandy. Hockney seems ever happier to be here. Besides the sketchbooks and the big panorama, he has made seven medium-sized paintings and a few portraits. One can measure the extent to which he takes his time to enter into his subject. One sees that it is an endless process of becoming ever more precise. The time spent approaching the sky, and the passion he now puts into it, indicate as much. He identifies clearly the challenges that he sets for himself and methodically takes them on, one after the other.

Recently, he has been busy preparing a new book to be published by Taschen: *My Window*. It consists of 120 drawings made in Los Angeles on an iPhone every morning upon waking, and sometimes in the evening... From his bed, David draws what he sees through the window. The sunrise or the sunset, the bouquet or pot of flowers that an attentive hand has placed for him on the windowsill and replaces with others after two or three days.

There are no new finished paintings in the studio. On the easel, only a painted sketch: a sky. It is in the same spirit as the structured skies surrounding the apple, pear, and quince trees. 'Are you going to paint a tree against this sky?' 'I don't know yet. I just wanted to capture this sky for itself. I did the painting outside, over there, while looking at the sky. You need to work fast because it changes all the time. I skipped lunch, so I could keep painting before that sky vanished.'

I had initially concluded that the first sky, the one with the apple tree, resulted from night-time thinking and not direct observation of the subject. I was wrong – it obviously resulted from both.

After hearing that the sky was painted from nature this time, I ask: 'Was this in order to capture the exact colour of the moment?'

David turns around, his eyes sparkling, and retorts: 'What is an exact colour?'

I think of Wittgenstein's remarks about colour. There is no exact colour, only the colour of the perceived sensation. In contrast, David explains that what he seeks when painting from nature is form; he strives to follow the forms that he sees in the sky. But there are no clouds today; for me, the sky is uniformly clear. Not for him. These circumvolutions, which are drawn by each brushstroke and recall Van Gogh's skies, are invented, yet not from nothing: he truly sees them. A sky is never a coat of uniform colour; it is transparent, deep, a space; you feel the depth of this space but you cannot tell how far it goes, how far you perceive it, and this is what needs to be rendered by painting on the flat surface of the canvas. The curved marks that let the white background of the canvas show through suggest this thickness and depth.

No century has painted the sky in this way. Yet if there is anything that, arguably, has not changed since the dinosaurs, it has to be the sky. There have always been clouds, fogs, sunrises and sunsets, big blue or grey skies, nearly clear skies and heavily-clouded ones, but every era has painted them differently because every era has seen them differently. Altdorfer's sky is not Claude Lorrain's sky, and Claude Lorrain's sky is not Turner's.

'When I was in Yorkshire, I lived by the sea. I didn't paint the sea, which didn't really interest me.

The countryside interestd me, the arrival of spring. I had to take the car to draw from nature. Here, I'm immersed in nature. I see the things that I paint, can look at them at all times. The more I look at them, the better I know and understand them. I have an immense sky before my eyes and it changes all the time. I didn't have that in Los Angeles. There, the weather stays the same the whole year; one hardly notices the seasons.'

***

28 October 2019.

The sky that was a mere painted sketch has found its subject: a group of trees at mid-distance in a foggy atmosphere. 'I had to work very fast to capture this sky before it vanished', he says. 'I skipped lunch.' One thinks of Monet at the window of the Savoy Hotel, on the lookout for effects of fog so that he can get back to painting the Charing Cross Bridge. I ask to see the subject, which is just to the right of the studio door, where there is a terrace with a table and a few chairs, and where Hockney sits smoking a cigarette, looking at what surrounds him.

***

12 November 2019.

Hockney has come to Paris to see the Bacon retrospective once again. It is Tuesday; the Pompidou Centre is closed. We meet at the Café Beaubourg with Jean Clair and his wife Laura. David chooses the canopied outdoor section of the café where one can smoke at leisure. It has begun to rain. The sound of the rain on the awning delights the guests, each of whom recounts their experience in Japan. The rain doubles in intensity and the wind almost becomes a gale.

'I hope that all the rain in the sky is not falling today. I began a landscape in the rain yesterday, and need to continue it tomorrow. If it doesn't rain anymore, I'm stuck. Rain is an interesting subject because it's complex. Photography has never managed to represent rain. A camera does not see the rain as we do. We see space through the rain, we see the rain in front of us and the rain in the distance. A camera flattens everything out.'

He continues: 'When *Singin' in the Rain* was being shot, the filmmakers realised that they weren't able to film the rain as they wished. Everything was done in the studio, with water sprinkled down on the actors from watering cans perched above them. The filmmakers then noticed that the camera could film the rain better if they mixed milk into the water. It's one of the five or six best movies in cinema history. *Entertainment*: isn't that the minimum requirement? Most people have forgotten that.'

Patrice Cotensin points out to me that the story is likely just a legend; but as a character quips at the end of John Ford's *The Man Who Shot Liberty Valance*, 'When the legend becomes fact, print the legend!'

David then takes a sketchbook from his pocket and holds it out to me. It is a new panorama made around his house, 'La Grande Cour', which he has painted with coloured inks from small brush pens. He has about a dozen of these pens in his pocket.

'It took me five days to do it.' Everything is built up from parallel lines and dots, in order to let the white of the paper filter through. It is not Divisionist Pointillism in the sense of divided colour, as Signac intended. The dots forming the path all have the same colour and their juxtaposition forms a texture. And this texture is alive. There is no sky;

the trees and hills stand out from the white background of the paper. It is the fourth concertina book on the same subject, and he intends to keep following the changing seasons.

We are the only visitors at the Bacon exhibition. The exhibition opens with the portrait of Jacques Dupin. I remember that Bacon did not want Dupin to sit for him. He asked him for a photograph. 'But not a nice one', he had added. 'Go to a photo booth, take a series of photos, and send me the worst of them – blurry, budged, botched, that's what I need.' The anecdote amuses Hockney. 'He was a bit sadistic, wasn't he? But also elegant, chic, even a little snobbish. Of course, everything comes from Picasso, but he's the only one to have taken that from Picasso because it's his own life that has gone into it.'

David looks for a long time at each painting, from up close and from afar. He asks for a wheelchair but does not want to be pushed; he moves along at his own rhythm using his feet.

The Boltanski retrospective opens this evening. I saw Christian at Café Beaubourg. 'You are coming this evening, aren't you?' he asks. But we have been given the opportunity to see the exhibition before it opens. I tell David about the circumstances of Christian Boltanski's birth, how his father, who had hidden under a wooden floor throughout the war, would come out only at night to join his wife. His parents had imitated a quarrel with screams and broken objects to let the neighbours and the concierge hear it. The next day, his mother told everyone that her husband had left and good riddance to him. That is how his father escaped the roundup.

Hockney takes a close interest in Boltanski's way of working – the accumulation, the occupation of space, the simplicity of the message. He says: 'He's the only French artist of his generation, isn't he? In any case, I know of no other.'

*

I receive a photograph of a new painting: five trees in the foreground, beyond the curve in the path where the white of the canvas represents rain puddles. In the background, a rising path bordered by a grey-blue hedge, from which a few poplars stand out against a cloudy, lively, grey sky. The horizon is luminous, formed by white dots above the hedge, which is reduced to an almost homogenous shadow. Is this the painting begun in the rain?

***

22 November 2019.

The painting is now finished. The rain can't really be seen. The violet tint of the road indicates that it is wet. I ask: 'Is there anything else that a camera cannot see as well as we do?' David thinks for a long time and replies: 'The sky. We see the depth of the sky. We see that a sky, even a uniformly blue one, is not a flat surface. Photography doesn't see this.

'And there's also the question of size. When you see a tree, you know whether it's big or small. But take a photo of it and, without a benchmark beside it, you cannot know if the tree is big or small. Stalin, who was short, insisted on being filmed or photographed from below. Who would believe that Kirk Douglas was short? He seems tall in all his films – but such is the cameraman's art, the art of lying.'

David shows me two new portraits of Celia. They will be the high point of the National Portrait Gallery exhibition. The last one is only a few monochromatic watercolour brushstrokes. Celia is smiling. 'I had to work very fast to capture the smile and the eyes at the same time. When one smiles, the eyes become smaller. And it's impossible to keep a smiling face naturally; it quickly freezes into a mask.'

Celia had come with Scarlett, one of her granddaughters, already an adult. David made a beautiful portrait of her. Doubtless, he was not seeking to recover a memory of Celia when she was young, in the way that he had painted her so well in the past – what filters through this portrait is the memory of another portrait, Olga as depicted by Picasso: the pose, the position of the head, the bearing, the oval face...

Suddenly, in a cheerful tone, he asks: 'Have you seen my disco lights?' He fetches a remote-control device and plunges the studio into darkness. Then he turns on big projectors, set up in the corners of the walls and aimed at the ceiling. They alternatively produce a blue, red, or yellow light. 'Watch how this changes the colours of the paintings.' It is like a fairy tale. The paintings seem alive. The red tile roofs of Beuvron become black or orange or suddenly a darker, denser red. In the landscapes, whole sections disappear while the colour in others is enhanced. Hockney, who has always known how to grasp the latest technological breakthroughs, has once again found a way of questioning our relationship to colour.

He plans to return in a few days with J.P. to Los Angeles, where they shall spend Christmas and January, and come back here in early February so as not to miss the arrival of spring. But, like last year, he shall miss the winter season. He is not a man who regrets. What most excites him is the spring, when he follows the order in which flowers and leaves appear: the narcissuses, the daffodils, the plums, the hawthorns, the apple trees and the pear trees. As in the trees, the sap appears to rise in him, making him do great things.

***

14 February 2020.

David has been back for a few days now, impatient

to resume his dialogue with the Norman countryside. This time, he readies himself so that spring will not go by without him. He already has a plan. He will do the cherry tree before its first flowers emerge, then once more when it blooms. In general, cherry trees are the first to blossom in the spring. In reality, plum trees bloom earlier; mine is already covered with flowers. But there are no plum trees on Hockney's property.

He has yet to begin painting in the studio again. I find him sitting at the dining-room table, in front of his iPad. He is drawing what he sees through the window: a tall leafless tree under a vast pale sky made up of a thousand tiny hachures that he has attenuated with white marks. He likes to make the sky vibrate; this is how he renders the wind, the depth of space. The iPad drawing vocabulary contains all the marks he needs for it. 'It is really a new medium, you can do things that you couldn't do otherwise.' He calmly continues to build up his landscape through little touches with his stylus as I look on. He adds one, then two trees in the distance. These poplars stand along the stream that flows at the end of the field. I have often told him that he should have the many mistletoe balls removed from those trees – a parasite that will end up killing them. His view is that the mistletoe balls define the space better than if they were not there; they form the last background before the horizon; he intends to paint them before thinking about saving his trees. To every man his priorities.

I ask him how the flight went. 'Eleven hours door to door', he says. 'From Burbank to Deauville. Burbank Airport is a twenty-minute drive from our house on Montcalm Avenue. There's no waiting to check in, no security, a direct private flight from Los Angeles to Deauville. Of course, it costs a fortune, but what else can I do with my money at my age except simplify my life and save time for painting? The landing was a little rough because we arrived in the middle of a storm.'

He had gone in for a medical check-up in Los Angeles – a scan for everything that can be scanned. Everything is fine. A light hormonal treatment as a precaution. He is a bit upset about the side effects, but adds with resignation: 'I'm eighty-two, it doesn't terribly matter.'

At the end of the morning, David suggests that we have lunch at the Café Forges in Beuvron. The entrance to the village is blocked by some renovation work being carried out on the square. 'Lucky I painted it in time', he says, 'it will never be how it was before.'

'I'd like the ox tongue', he tells the waitress in perfect French, 'and a bottle of cider.' He explains that his early deafness has prevented him from learning foreign languages: what he hears is not distinct enough for him to memorise it. On the other hand, his exceptionally acute vision may be a partial compensation for the deafness.

***

24 February 2020.

Preview of the *Drawing from Life* exhibition at the National Portrait Gallery in London. Just as the English have a liking for, and a tradition of, written biographies (a genre in which they excel better than any other people), they also show an especial devotion to painted portraits, to the extent that an entire museum is dedicated to this art: the National Portrait Gallery, in Trafalgar Square, next to the National Gallery. Works there are preserved not so much for their art historical importance as for the portrayed personality's prominence in the nation's history. There, one finds the Tudors, the Stuarts, and so on. Out of their pride in this great contemporary British portraitist, the museum has organised an exhibition: *Drawing from Life*. The exhibition consists of portraits of the five subjects David Hockney has portrayed most often: Celia Birtwell, his longtime friend; Gregory Evans, who was his closest friend and then his collaborator; Maurice Payne, the master engraver with whom the artist has made some of his most beautiful prints; Laura Hockney, the artist's mother, ever ready to sit for her son; and, finally, the artist himself, who has many times given himself over to the tradition of self-portraiture.

All of the models are present, save his mother, who is no longer living. The exhibition gathers drawings in pencil, charcoal, and ink that have been made over a fifty-year period. The viewer witnesses how the subjects evolve and age; and one can see how the artist's emotions evolve with respect to the subject. It is a silent novel, and yet how voluble. Gregory, slouching and disenchanted, is no longer the handsome youth tenderly sketched a few years back. Maurice's eagle-like profile has remained on the lookout. Celia, who is now a plump little old lady, keeps her smile on to face the ravages of time. When she was young, wearing her black silk slip, it was less her smile than a dreamy look that lent her an air of mystery.

Hockney was keen on adding two or three recent portraits of each model to round out the exhibition (excepting his mother, of course). They are grouped together in the last room, which thus takes on the atmosphere of the Guermantes' salon, where we find the characters of an entire lifetime. To Celia, who has kept a touch of vanity and was worried about being painted as an old lady, Hockney responds: 'Yes, an old lady painted by a very old gentleman.' Gregory, the handsome youth, is slumped in an armchair, seemingly depressed. Maurice's Beckettian face has grown gaunter still. The self-portraits show us multiple aspects of the artist's personality.

The next day, a preview of the portrait exhibition at Annely Juda Fine Art. There are large charcoal drawings on canvas, which I had seen in Los Angeles, and a few drawings on paper from Normandy. Celia once again; Margaret; Scarlett, who resembles Olga; Jonathan's son Matthew. For dinner, David Juda has had a big table set in the middle of the gallery. Celia is there with her granddaughter. I sit across from Kasmin and next to Norman Rosenthal. Edith Devaney, of the Royal Academy, questions me about Normandy...

***

17 March 2020.

France has come to a standstill; the orders are to stay home. We remain in Beuvron. Hockney asks how we are doing. He is a little worried about the situation, but thinks that he is probably better protected in Rumesnil, far from everything, than anywhere else. He needs only to remain in his studio. What could be better? He congratulates himself on not being locked down in Los Angeles.

Nearly every day, I receive a new image created on his iPad. Since returning from London, he has yet to retake possession of the painting studio – he is too preoccupied with the flowers blooming one after the other. The iPad enables him to work more quickly.

The large pear tree with its fallen branch. Art history tells us that landscape painting begins when figures leave the site. Here, the figure makes a comeback: a tree in all its majesty. *Standing Figure*, like a king or, here, a wounded warrior. But it is a figure against a background. Here we are again. And the tree defies perspective. Some branches move towards us while others head into the background, not respecting the laws of optical perspective.

Kenneth Clark speaks of Constable, the techniques that he used – separate touches, little white zebra stripes made with a palette knife – ever searching for the sense of dramatic unity: the subordination of countless visual data to a single pictorial idea. I can think only of Constable and Hockney who have known how to give such majesty to trees. Perhaps also Corot, but that is less certain. 'The envelope of light', Corot would say. Once it is found, the painting is there. All that is anecdotal vanishes.

The invention of landscape is the invention of the marks of which it consists, and which make a painting. In most of these drawings and paintings, Hockney has not made a landscape; he has made the portrait of a tree that stands front and centre, imposing, solitary, taking up all the space of the canvas in majesty.

***

23 April 2020.

Although he lives only five minutes away, I have not paid a visit to David since 15 March. That is, since France was in lockdown. We telephone each other. All the restaurants are closed. He was a regular at simple restaurants in Bonnebosq, Beuvron, and Manerbe. He likes hearty popular dishes: tripe, chitterlings, sweetbread, frog legs. Now he is reduced to sandwiches prepared for him by Jean-Pierre.

Another effect of the lockdown: he has nothing to read anymore. I take out a few English titles from my personal library: the poems of Emily Dickinson and T. S. Eliot, Boswell's *Life of Samuel Johnson*, *Moby Dick*, a few Conrad novels, including *The Secret Sharer* and *Heart of Darkness*, and Gertrude Stein's *Tender Buttons*. I leave them on his doorstep.

Yesterday I asked David if he had pinned the printed proofs of his iPad drawings to the wall in order to see them all together. This morning, I receive photographs showing J.P. and Jonathan covering the wall; they have been taken by David, who can be seen in the cheval glass to the side. I tell him how impatient I am to see the drawings. He responds: 'All you have to do is come over. Enough of this lockdown. In any event, smokers are protected, it's proven.' At 4 p.m., I am there. The big studio wall, which must be at least 30 metres in length, is covered with printouts of all the iPad drawings that he has made since his return from Los Angeles – at least one per day. They are pinned to the wall in chronological order. Which is to say, in the first ones, it is still winter: tall bare trees, their structures unfolding, with moonlight or pale sunrises behind the poplars; then arrive the first flowers, and then the leaves. He often depicts the same tree seen from the same spot after an interval of a few weeks. Thus, in the same way that the portraits made of Celia or Gregory over a period of 50 years mark the passage of time – the time of a human life – another passage of time is palpable here: the cyclical time of seasons and renewal in contrast to the irreversible time of human life. It is what is happening deliberately here: the cycle of the seasons unrolling like the conquest of England on the Bayeux Tapestry. The iPad is particularly well adapted to this project. David shows me how he uses it. The software offers a range of different structuring marks: dots, crosses, stars, etc. Cursors enable him to choose the desired scale, the spacing between the marks, their thickness, their density... A prismatic colour wheel allows him to select the desired colour from all its various shades. The speed, softness, and force of the stylus stroke modifies the mark as would a brushstroke. One can even make seemingly random splotches and splashes. When he decides to paint a given tree at a new stage in the season, David goes back to the structure of the bare tree in the winter season, adding flowers or leaves to it. His project is to show change, the passage of time, and this can be seen all the better when it is based on the same structure, the same tree, seen from the same spot, in the same scale. The surest approach in this case is indeed to start again with the winter drawing of the tree and its immutable structure. And it is enabled by the iPad. He shows me how the movement of a finger swathes everything in fog. 'It took me some time to capture the morning fog', he says, 'but I captured it. And the sunrise... You need to work fast. Ten minutes go by and it's already something else.' One can measure how complex this learning process with the subject is, and how the work on the iPad will inform the work on the painting to follow, whose rhythm cannot be the same. It is as if he has needed to tame the landscape, getting to know its moods, its demands, before finally becoming its master. 'The desire to seize forms out of the world man endures', as Malraux writes, 'in order to bring them into the world he governs.' The invention of landscape is the invention of the marks of which it consists, and which make a painting. These marks never existed – nor will they ever exist – in nature; they belong to the category of painting, abstractions, mental constructions, imaginary lines and forms, which build another reality and another category. Just as the physicist describes a phenomenon by using equations, a painter translates reality by intermingling invented signs placed on a surface. This has been known for a long time; nothing is new here. But the work with the iPad software makes this even clearer. The iPad even enables one to scroll through – which David does in front of me – the film of how the image was constructed, mark by mark; everything has been saved, and this film can be viewed as it moves forwards or backwards, slowly or quickly; it can be stopped wherever one wishes to examine a step in the process. It is fascinating.

These drawings will have to be printed for the exhibition, and we discuss the scale; two or three formats will probably be needed. The close-ups, such as the bouquet of daffodils or the branch of the cherry tree in blossom, will have to be preserved on the present scale – larger than nature, but not overly so. On the other hand, the big trees that stand alone, like kings or warriors, will surely need to be printed on a greater scale to convey their majesty, the force emanating from them.

***

28 April 2020.

This is how we want to show them. I receive an e-mail with this subject line containing a presentation of the images, enlarged in three formats, mounted as if they were hanging on the wall. They are presented chronologically, from the end of winter to the explosion of spring. The big cherry tree is seen first with bare branches, then with its first blossoms, then, at long last, in full bloom, like an enormous bouquet of cotton on a large trunk; and then in the budding of its first leaves, of a tender green that will not last long. We go to Rumesnil that very evening to see the wall in person. About 85 images have been pinned up in double rows along three walls. The complete line-up must be no less than 50 metres in length. This is when we finally and truly see that the project, pondered ever since that first visit to Bayeux, has resulted in painting *The Arrival of Spring* like Queen Matilda's tapestry. But from Bayeux to Cabourg-Balbec is not such a stretch, and William the Conqueror, whose fleet set out from Dives, must have run into Marcel Proust as he was crossing the bridge leading to the harbour. When one walks along David Hockney's wall, it is not merely a landscape that unfurls before one's eyes, as was the case with the 360-degree panorama; it is indeed time itself that flows by. Hockney has long been sensitive and attentive to time in painting. In his view, it is what photography seriously lacks. I remember that when we first met, at the preview of his first photographic collages at Kasmin's in London, I spontaneously began the conversation by mentioning Proust and the passage of time; this is what his collages had immediately suggested to me. It is crucial to bring time into a work of art, simply because time is life. The cause of death is birth. The only permanent thing is change. From sameness to sameness, the sameness becomes something else. One sees this in portraits like in nature. The miracle of spring is that it marks a renewal each time. And no one is ready to forget the spring of 2020. Like the plague year in London told by Daniel Defoe, or the cholera of *The Horseman on the Roof*. I have just read these two books and I mention them during our conversation. David has read the Defoe and remembers it well. 'It's not a journal written directly about the event', he says, 'but a reconstruction written a few dozen years later.' Be this as it may, 2020, in collective memory, will ever remain the virus year… and the year of David Hockney's Normandy series, *The Arrival of Spring*.

***

3 May 2020.

Heavy slanting rainfall nearly all day long. Hockney immediately seizes on it: the glistening road that crosses the lawn, trees and coppices, the distant line of hills in the fog, and the rain, from the top to the bottom of the image, depicted in imperfectly parallel slanting brushstrokes. Something remarkable: the colour of the rain is not the same when back-dropped by the grey sky or the green lawn. Nothing could be more normal, of course, as water is translucid. Whereas the brushstrokes representing the rain are more or less the same grey as the sky, those falling across the green lawn are milky white.

He opens his iPad and shows me how he has just animated this image. The rain can be seen falling from top to bottom against the background of the landscape. This is one of the features specific to the iPad: brushstrokes representing rain can be selected and animated. Hokusai and Hiroshige would have loved it.

In another video, I see the big cherry tree evolving, from bare branches to flowers and then to leaves, over the course of just a few seconds. One understands why Hockney keeps the structure of the tree, seen in winter, to dress it in flowers and then in leaves, instead of re-drawing everything. He uses all that the iPad makes possible. At one moment in the video, the tree suddenly shrinks on the screen, as though sinking into the landscape. Because the tree has grown with its leaves and new spring budding. Hockney needs more space around the tree to draw it. Nothing is simpler. With the iPad, if you need to increase the margins to continue your drawing, no problem. 'It's an endless sheet of paper.' Degas would have loved it, for he often had to add strips of paper to continue a drawing that had taken him beyond the initial sheet.

I spot a new composition on the wall that had not been photographed and sent to me by e-mail. It is very different from all the others: in the foreground, the meadow with dandelion flowers and the downy balls that the lady on the Larousse logo blows on, whose seeds are sown to the winds; branches and leaves, some of them haloed with yellow trimming indicating that they are lit by the sun; through the branches, a distant tree painted in blue. Unsurprised by the colour, I ask what and where the tree is. 'It's that one', replies Hockney, 'the first one you see from the studio door. It's green, of course, but I need contrast so I painted it blue.'

Following Franz Marc's blue horse and Matisse's blue nude, we now have Hockney's blue tree.

***

7 May 2020.

I receive a night landscape under a full white moon. The light is so strong that the sky itself is not black, but dark blue, and the trees project long shadows moving towards us. A moment later, I receive an e-mail: 'Did you see the moon last night?' Indeed, Françoise had awakened me in the middle of the night so I could admire it. It was as though we were in broad daylight. I looked into the cause of the phenomenon and found that the moon was at its perigee yesterday – at its closest distance from the earth, approximately 50,000 kilometres closer than at its apogee. It is called a 'super Flower Moon' (American Indians associate it with the blooming of wildflowers in May). I read in a newspaper that the moon that night was 14% bigger and 30% brighter than usual. I ask David when exactly he made this drawing. 'At four in the morning. As soon as I opened my eyes, I saw the exceptional light, so I snatched up the iPad to keep a trace of it.' Another advantage of the technology: one need not turn on an electric light to draw, as the light on the screen suffices for one to see the drawing and does not modify the luminosity of the subject. By any other traditional means, the canvas or the sheet of paper must be illuminated to see the marks that one places on it.

That evening we visit the studio, and discover a large-format version of the full moon over La Grande Cour. Seeing a white dot in the lefthand corner of the sky, Françoise says: 'The star – it was there, I saw it.' 'Yes', says David, 'It's Venus. I need to make it a little brighter.'

The Arrival of Spring series is nearing its end. David declares that he still wants to make five or six iPad drawings before returning to painting.

A part of the house or an open doorway can be seen in several of the images. The human presence, the invisible observer, can be sensed even more strongly there. When an architectural element is in the landscape, especially if it is in the foreground, it is almost as though we could hear the observer breathing. Like the Narrator of *In Search of Lost Time*, he withdraws, but everything emanates from him.

I have brought from Paris my English copy of *In Search of Lost Time*. David has long wished to reread it, and this is the ideal time and place to do so. I remember finding Scott Montcrieff's translation, which appeared during the author's lifetime, particularly elegant. It nonetheless had to be revised. Montcrieff perfectly renders Proust's sinuous sentences, but he sometimes misses the meaning of the colloquial, even slang, expressions, especially when they have a double entendre – usually a bawdy one. David is amused by the anecdote.

One image is altogether different from the others: a close-up of the meadow with neither sky nor horizon, as if the horizontality of the subject were fictively abolished and raised into a frontal image. There is no scale, as if we were in a jungle. Is it the word jungle that makes me think of Le Douanier Rousseau? When I mention this to David, he says: 'Edith Devaney told me that it reminded her of the *Lady and the Unicorn* tapestry.' Edith is absolutely right: the lawn of the *Lady and the Unicorn*, with its scattered flowers and leaves surging up like geysers, possesses the same dreamlike freshness.

***

30 May 2020.

'Come and see our swimming pool, it will have yellow lines on it by six.' The injunction arrives by e-mail with a photograph. In front of the house, there is a kind of concrete foundation on which the previous owners had installed a movable plastic basin, a swimming pool for children. David had the basin removed, and painted the concrete with blue and yellow lines imitating movements on the water's surface and reflections of sunlight. 'It's the first swimming pool sculpture', he says.

We have an aperitif in front of the pond at sunset. A moorhen is paddling on the water between the duck decoys; the toads are making a deafening racket. A low sun filters through the willow branches. David has not had us sit here by chance. It is the exact subject of his most recent iPad drawing and the same time of day. Looking through the back-lit willow, we can set our eyes on the sun. David says: 'There was a little wooden fence in front of the pond, do you remember? I never drew it because it bothered me. When I drew the pond, I pretended it wasn't there so I could better see the landscape. In the end, I had it removed. It's better this way, isn't it? The previous owners had small children; it was a protection. I don't need it.'

There are now more than 110 images of the spring in the studio. The project is nearing its conclusion. This spring has been extraordinarily fertile. The responsiveness of the iPad, the fact that it can be carried everywhere like a sketchbook, the great mastery that David has acquired of this technique, combined with his appetite for the subject – it has all enabled him to accumulate images as never before. And this series has been pushed much further, becoming more complex and inventive than *The Arrival of Spring* in Yorkshire. Without leaving the house and with the tablet as his only tool, he has made a world surge forth: the rising of the sap, the blossoming of the flowers, the growth of the leaves and their transformation from tender to dark green… No one had ever attempted it before. Perhaps Stravinsky, with other means.

The Royal Academy of Arts in London has offered to exhibit the entire set next spring. Cécile Debray, who has come to visit, would like to show them all at the Orangerie in autumn 2021.

'Another advantage of the iPad', remarks David, 'is that you don't need to clean the brushes when the session is over. You find your palette fresh and clean the next morning. And even at night… I take the iPad to bed with me and keep working. I've never had the possibility of working all the time. For an artist, the lockdown is a godsend.'

The last image: the branch of a cherry tree with a few red cherries on it. Even though the solstice is three weeks away, summer is already there. The world is coming out of lockdown little by little. We shall long remember the spring of 2020. (David never pronounces 'two thousand twenty', but always 'twenty twenty'!)

I ask David if he really intends to continue *The Arrival of Spring* series until 21 June, the last day of the season. 'No, I don't', he replies, 'it's already summer, isn't it?' The weather, indeed, is all aestival. 'I want to start painting again. I will turn some of these images into paintings. I have a good grasp of the subject now...' 'Do you know which images you want to transpose into painting?' 'Yes, I do.'

I ask no more questions.

One chapter ends, another begins.

David has already drawn the final scene. Like an intertitle in a silent film, against an apple-green background framed by a dancing frieze, he has written in coloured letters:

THE END (Fin)
of springtime 2020
It was very exciting
I'll be back next year
LOVE LIFE David H.